T0069716

How Do Seeds Travel?

Isabella Masani

Seed

Plant

New Plant

New plants grow from seeds.
Sometimes a new plant grows beside
the plant that dropped the seeds.

2

Sometimes seeds travel far away before they grow into plants.
How do seeds travel?

Seed

Plant

Seeds from this plant look like this.
How will these seeds travel far away?

Traveling Seed

New Plant

The wind will carry the seeds.
When the wind stops, the seeds will fall.
Then a new plant will grow.

5

Seed

Plant

Seeds from this plant look like this.
How will these seeds travel far away?

6

Traveling Seed

New Plant

The sea will carry the seeds.
The sea will wash the seeds onto the shore.
Then a new plant will grow.

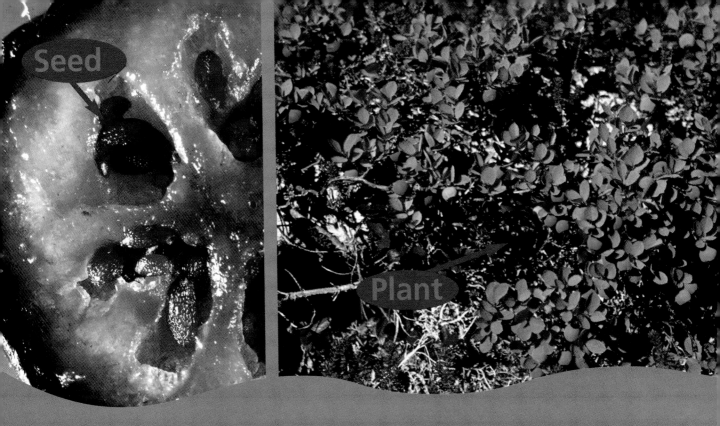

Seeds from this plant look like this.
How will these seeds travel far away?

Traveling Seed

New Plant

Animals will eat the seeds in berries.
The seeds will fall in the animals' droppings.
Then a new plant will grow.

Seed

Plant

Seeds from this plant look like this.
How will these seeds travel far away?

New Plant

Traveling
Seed

An animal's fur will carry the seeds.
The seeds stick to the fur until they fall off.
Then a new plant will grow.

How will these seeds travel far away?